Ruminate

Holly Meaden

BookLeaf
Publishing

India | USA | UK

Presentation by *BookLeaf Publishing*

Web: www.bookleafpub.com

E-mail: info@bookleafpub.com

ISBN: 9789358319675

First edition 2024

PREFACE

There is nothing particularly extraordinary here.
Just some feelings and a few words on paper.

Delicate Little Thing

This delicate little thing.
Brushing my finger on the back of your hand.
It is walking away and looking back.
It is meeting eyes when we say goodbye
It is a morning when I look at you and get shy.
Knowing you are nervous when you eat
It is watching where you point your feet.
It is half a sugar not two.
It is looking at the door waiting for you.
It is hearing a laugh across a room.
It is grinning from ear to ear at the thought of
you.
This delicate little thing might shatter.
And all these tiny moments will no longer
matter.
You might not notice a drop in an April shower.
But for a moment in time, this delicate little
thing held all the power.

Psychic

I'm not saying I'm going mad
But I literally asked a Pyshic for a helping hand.
They told me crap but it helped me relax.
And now my bank account is sad.

Funnier

Why aren't I funnier?
Of all the traits I'm lacking the one I just can't
mend.
The gift of talk was never my thing
I tend to do, more than speak, and think more
than do.
Why aren't I funnier?
More like you.
To make you break a smile and let out a chuckle
is all I want to do.
But I can't and I shan't and it makes me sad to
think.
Why aren't I funnier?

Thoughts I had on the stairs but you already left.

I said the wrong thing.
Everyone has once said something they
shouldn't.
It's that age old mistake.
One usually men make.
Although any gender can make a mistake.
And I'm replaying it in my head
When she sat their excitedly but I said.
Why did I say that when what I really meant.

You look lovelier than a sunset in June after a
lifetime of December.

Wild Afternoons

Afternoon sunshine haze.
Not too far past one.
There's Natts in the air.
We acknowledge but we don't care.
On a porch swing light peaking through the
brim.
My arms around you, your head on my chest.
I recite Dickenson and you just listen.
She said wild nights I say wild afternoons.
Little pitter from the fouantain blue tits on the
fence.
Ferns sway in the breeze.
Your palm over my knees.
You look up at me.
And I think I'm in a dream.

The Jay

Sitting down to toast and tea.
Another normal daily routine.
Overcast a mix of grey a rainy fine haze.
I caught a flash of the most brilliant blue I'd ever
seen.
On the fence before me was a lifer.
With feathers my favourite colour.
I spent the next summer with treats galore.
To capture a photo of a bird I had never seen
before.
And that bird became my white whale.
The start of a twitching tale.
How all of a sudden out of the blue.
You're chasing feathers and wondering which Tit
are you?
Well, it all started with a Jay on a fence and a
daily routine.

Alone

Some time alone, alone just me.
Sometime alone, in the muddied sea.
With laughter, alone fiddling piano.
Feet beating the street alone, so, so,
Under a thousands leafes moving slow.
I can sit with a thought or two or three.
Something few dare to achieve.
So when I'm alone I'm actually free.
To transverse my mind like a map.
And all I come up with is cat.

The Rook

She sang me a song so sweet.
I searched for a black bird.
Around the room and under my seat.
What I found on the ground.
Fell short of that sweet sound.
See that woman was a rook.
And she started to caw,
That shut another door.

Origami

It's a shame how you bend and fold like paper to suit someone else's needs.
Yet standing there before me you are the finest sculpture
And all we seem to do is bend and fold like paper.
And sooner or later we will pull apart from the centre.
Life doesn't get easier if your folds are straighter.
We all disintegrate and float away like paper.
Next time fold into a daffodil and save me for later.
Holding on tight to you, but it weaps we are only paper.
Do not be a second choice wait for me to envelop you
At the dance with confetti, this night is going to wash away
Please don't fold and bend again to suit his needs.
Be a sculpture. We are not oragami this life is only paper.

Folding Chair

She said "Oh to collapse like a folding chair and
be carried off in your arms"
She never wanted to know why where or how
Only that we must go, and we must go now.

The Letter

The intricacy of a hand penning a letter so
sweet.
The pages unfold from there envelope with an
absorbing scent.
The honey suckle that climbed the fence a spring
before.
All gone as the shredded paper hits the floor.

The Chatter

I want to be alone.
Comepletely, wholly, isolated.
Only then will I feel better.
Only then can my mind quiet the noise of man.
I don't want the lights on, I don't want the door
left unlocked.
I want a dark room and a quiet heart.
I want candle light and shadows on the walls.
Only then will I hear my own voice instead of
yours.
Only then can my mind quiet the noise of
woman.
I want to be alone.

Pine Cone

Pine cone tumbling through the mud,
Under orange trees.
Each thump with the toe cap
Springs it free.
Not bound to me nor bound in place.
Each crack of my boot the pine cone displaced.
From under the yew,
Travelling far from the green.
The conifers are but an aspirational dream.
Where the path stops your journey will end.
Be it unfavourable or just right,
Maybe little pine cone,
You will spring to life.

Autumn

The sun falls like a blanket on the patchwork
fields
Caresesss the blades green still Stubborn to
autumns chill
Fragile the fern first to turn embraces blades of
honey
Pacing for the dying light this autumn

The Fisherman

Knuckles white clenching a cap
A gift, a token a treasured possession
The sea filling the gaps in this woolen sweater
Heavy sinking darker into her trap
Boots like lead

Swirling turbulent skies smokey clouds pierced
violet and white
Salt fueled pellets hammering his cheek
Forced to be brave turn the Stern towards the
waves
Razor burn threads around his wrist Bowline
knot inches before clenched fist
To make a living to earn a wage nets cut loose
ghosts they've been made
The jib did whip, the bowl dips and as the hull
quakes the horses have their way

Sea filling the holes of vermilion woollen
sweater
Inhospitable bitter squeezes the lungs like a
trigger
Lips tingle mouthing profanity a dead letter
He never thanked him for the cap

A small consolation what the mind can see when
it ceases to sqirm
I assure you he always knew, and he will
eternally miss you

Old Fashioned Clocks

The left ear ticks whilst the right ear tocks
I love the sound of old fashioned clocks
Reminds me that time can never be stuck
This phase will end of being down on my luck
Yet in the back of my mind I know one day
I'll not hear that tick tock and long for a time
when nothing was okay

Confession

What a shame, we are all hiding.
The one thing the world could do with more of.
We die on that sword a thousand times and call it noble.
Maybe in temper and rage its worthy of a knighthood
But in love and kindness it's outright misunderstood.
There's no humiliation in love.
And those lucky enough to know should learn the art of a gentle let go.
Without contempt or retaliation.
Do not shatter the heart of another person
Just say you cannot be moved to feel the same
And let their burning flame turn to an ember and ease their pain.
And you.
I leave you with this.
A confession of love for want in return was never really love at all.

Anger

When you sit in anger too long
You may never find forgiveness
It's too late for some people
Their apologies are like salt
It is who they are not just what they do
I never want to raise my voice like a scary kids
cartoon
You might never mean to hurt me
And I never you
But being human my darling,
It's all we seem to do.

I Stand

The wheat waves without hurry
As the sun sears it's mark into my neck
And as the skin begins to turn a pale red
I stand
The swallows dart with effortless grace and
vanish below the brow
And as I am bathed in a summer eve
I stand
If a thought was to slip the stream of my
subconscious and into the forefront of my mind
it would be of you and yet
I stand
The breeze tingles the skin along my finger to
the base of my knuckles
As the rolled sleeves of my shirt ruffle at the
shoulder
I stand
As the time ticks down to the end of another
glorious day
There's very little I can do to cushion the
thoughts of you and so,
I stand
With a natural plaster of remarkable nature on
this land
I stand

Sun and Star

When you're trying to find beauty in November.
The easiest place to look is at her.
Easier said than done when you're a star and
she's the sun.
She reads by my light at night whilst I bathe in
her warmth in the day
We are one but we are not the same.
We can never tell this tale from the same page.
And like a primitive tribe I still worship and
scribe poems and make sacrafice.
Reckless to say I love the sun anyway.
Even if we can never shine the same.

Medium

I wish I could express myself in some form of
medium
My poems fall short, my piano is defective, my
words inaudible even though I'm screaming.
You're the only one that has me dreaming.
I look at her how I look at sunsets
And she looks at me like I have no meaning.
Curse this wretched heart to never follow it's
head instead.
Do not fall willingly into dark eyes but turn to
brighter skies.
 No need to pick up pen and write.
She's not flipping blind.
If she cannot see your hearts in the right place.
Then rip up this pretentious page.
There is no form of medium to tell you.
I love you.